PUPPETS WITH PIZAZZ

Can·Make·and·Do Books

PUPPETS WITH PIZAZZ

52 Finger and Hand Puppets Children Can Make and Use

by Joy Wilt
Gwen Hurn
John Hurn

Photographs by John Hurn

CREATIVE RESOURCES
Waco, Texas

PUPPETS WITH PIZAZZ

Acknowledgments

We wish to express our hearty thanks to Kathee Dayvolt for her marvelous help in the writing, editing, and typing of the manuscript.

We also thank Dan Jagt, Dona Hodge, Richard Doyle, and Michael Yale for their fine photographic lab work.

Lastly, we thank Stephanie Crawford for creating a puppet especially for this book.

Contents

About Puppets

A puppet is a figure of a person, animal, or object that is made to move by the efforts of a human being—child or adult. It derives its "life" and "personality" from that person's efforts and imagination.

Puppets belong in a child's world because they are:
 —fun
 —educational
 —entertaining

Puppets have the potential to
 —stimulate a child's *imagination*
 —provide ways in which a child can express his *creativity*
 —assist a child in *expressing* his thoughts and feelings
 —help a child develop his *listening* and *verbal* and language skills
 —give a child opportunities to use and develop his *small muscles*
 —provide opportunities for *socialization* in which children are constructively planning, working, and playing together

Puppets can be used specifically
 —as an art or craft project
 —to tell or dramatize a story
 —to teach facts or concepts
 —to play musical instruments or sing songs

—to recite poems, facts, Bible verses
—to ask and/or answer questions
—to impart information
—to make announcements
—to distribute prizes
—to give directions and/or instructions
—for role playing
   etc., etc., etc.

These puppets can be made and used at
—home
—school
—church
—social functions
—recreation programs

Puppets are categorized on the basis of how they move. Generally speaking, puppets are moved by a person's fingers or hands, or by strings or rods. If a puppet is moved by a person's fingers, it is called a "finger puppet." If it is moved by a person's hand, it is called a hand puppet, and so on. Marionettes, of course, are string puppets. Miscellaneous puppets that do not fit into any of these categories are generally referred to as "novelty puppets."

This book is the first in a series of three books on Puppetry. It specializes in hand and finger puppets, while the second book deals with rod, string, and novelty puppets; and the third with puppet stages and props.

The puppets that we recommend are simple enough to be made by children. We believe children should not only be allowed but encouraged to make their own puppets. It is our experience that anything a child makes seems to have more meaning to him. It is our experience also that a child will find it easier to use a puppet that he has made himself; generally speaking, it is easier for a child to create a character than it is for him to adapt himself to one. Not the least important reason for children to make their own puppets is the pride and sense of satisfaction they derive from having made something themselves.

We want to emphasize that the pictures and patterns provided in this book are merely ideas and suggestions. They should be used as guidelines only. The child should be encouraged to individualize his own puppet by modifying the basic idea or pattern in any way he chooses. The important thing for the child is not to reproduce a puppet from this book but rather to create his very own puppet.

JOY WILT

Finger Puppets

Finger-Face Puppet

1. Wrap a piece of lace around your index finger below the first joint. Glue the ends of the lace together.

You will need: Lace
White glue
Pen

2. Draw a girl's face on the ball of your finger to complete the puppet.

Kleenex Puppet

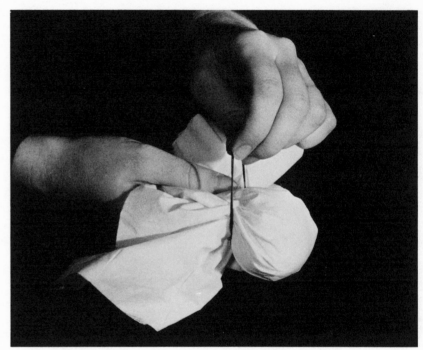

1. Place approximately four cotton balls in the center of an extra-large facial tissue.

2. Wrap the tissue around the cotton to form a round head. Use a rubber band to hold the tissue in place.

You will need: Cotton
Kleenex, extra-large size
Rubber band
Felt marker

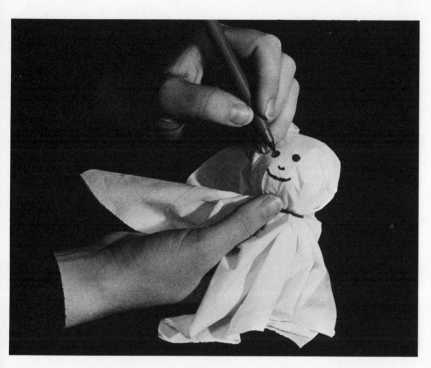

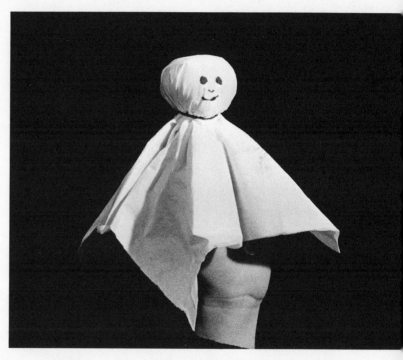

3. With a felt-tip pen, draw the facial features on the head.

4. Place your index finger through the rubber band and slightly into the head; allow the remaining tissue to cover your hand. Your puppet is now ready for use.

Tab Wraparound

1. First, make a tagboard duplicate of pattern 1. Use the duplicate to trace the pattern onto construction paper. Cut out the figure and decorate it with felt markers.

You will need: Tagboard   Scissors
                      Pen or pencil   Felt markers
                      Construction paper   Scotch tape

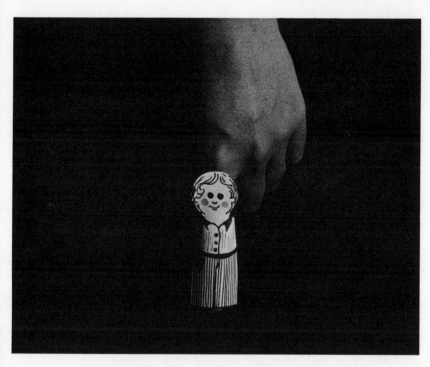

2. Wrap the arms behind the figure, around the index finger. Hold them in place and secure with a piece of Scotch tape.

Loop Wraparound

1. Make a tagboard duplicate of pattern 2. Trace the pattern outline onto a piece of construction paper and cut it out.

2. Cut a short strip of construction paper and form it into a loop that will fit snugly around your index finger. Glue the ends of the paper together.

3. Glue the loop to the back of the animal.

4. With felt markers, draw on the appropriate features. Now, insert your index finger through the loop and your puppet is complete.

Felt Wraparound

1. Cut out two strips of felt, one pink and one of any other color. Wrap the pink felt piece around your index finger to form a cylinder; then glue the edges together.

2. Keeping the pink felt cylinder on your finger, wrap the other piece of felt around it, lower edges together. Glue the two felt pieces together. **Important:** The strips must be glued while on your finger. If the pieces are glued on a flat surface they will buckle when wrapped.

You will need: Felt, pink and one other
color
Scissors
White glue
Rickrack

3. Next, cut out the appropriate facial features on felt and glue them onto the puppet.

4. Decorate with rickrack or similar adornment to complete your puppet.

23

Glove Finger Puppet

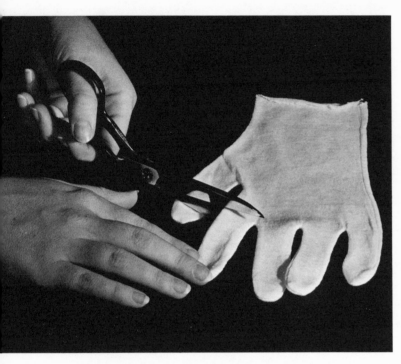

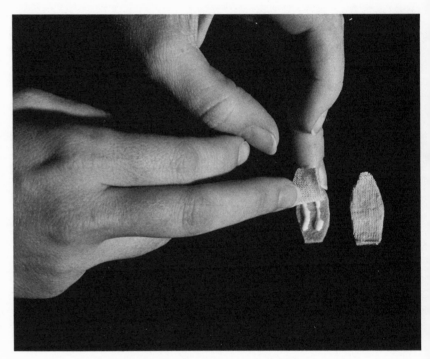

1. With a pair of scissors, remove the index finger from a white glove. (Inexpensive white cotton gloves are available at most photo dealers.)

2. Next, cut two pieces in the shape of rabbit ears from another part of the glove and two pieces from felt. Glue the cotton ears to the felt ears.

24

You will need: White glove   Fringe ball
                     Scissors   Plastic eyes
                     Felt   Dazzle bead
                     White glue   Pen

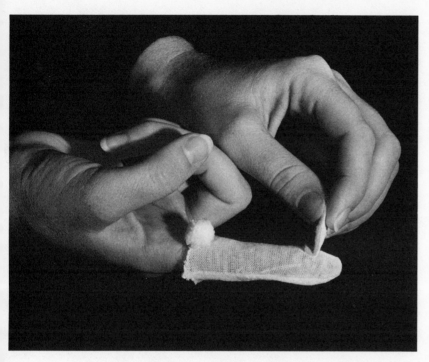

3. Glue the ear pieces to the glove finger, and attach a fringe ball for a tail.

4. Complete your puppet by adding small plastic eyes and a dazzle bead for the nose.

Glove Puppet with Caps

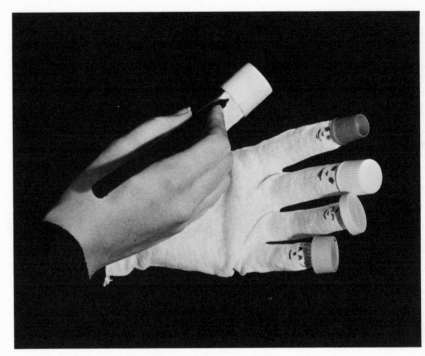

1. Place a white glove on one hand. With your other hand, glue small caps of various shapes and sizes to each finger.

2. Next, with a felt-tip pen, draw a face on each finger just below the cap.

You will need: *White glove*   *Small caps of various*
                    Felt-tip pen   *shapes and sizes (e.g.,*
                    White glue   *toothpaste, shampoo,*
                    deodorant, fingernail
                    polish)

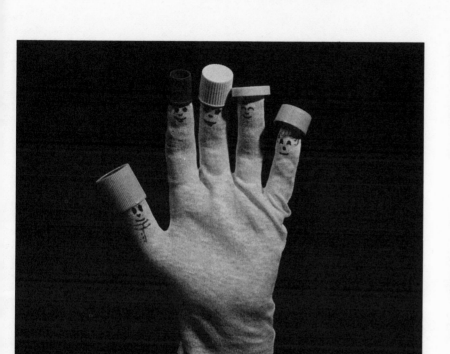

3. Hold the glove upright; there are now
five little puppets, each with a unique
hat.

Four-Finger Puppet

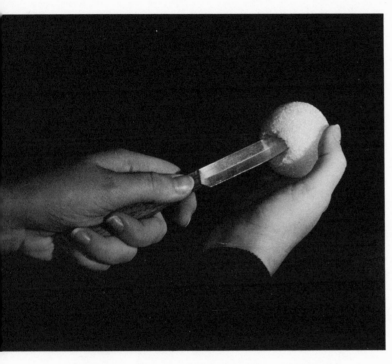

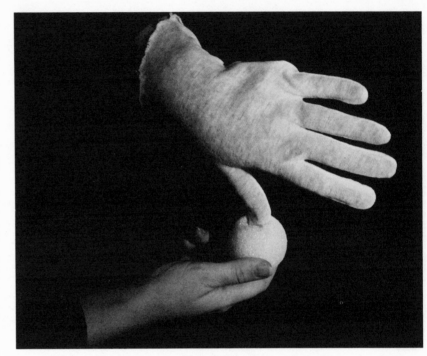

1. With a sharp knife, cut a hole large enough for your thumb in a 2″ styrofoam ball.

2. Put on the white glove. Glue the styrofoam ball to the thumb of the glove.

You will need:
Knife
2″ styrofoam ball
White glove

White glue
Felt
Plastic eyes

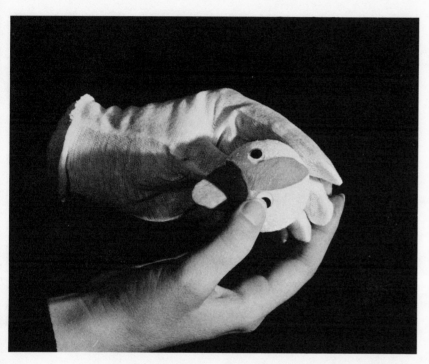

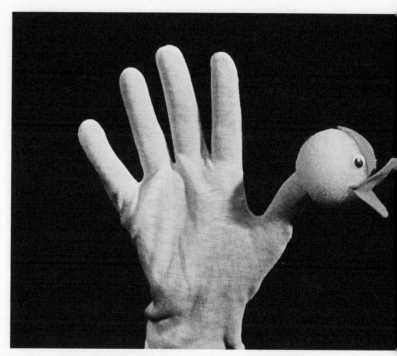

3. Now, add felt pieces and plastic eyes to the styrofoam ball to make it look like a duck's head.

4. Hold the glove as shown above; the fingers represent the duck's feathers.

Styrofoam Cup Puppet

1. Use a ball-point pen to draw a face on a styrofoam cup. Make a circle about the size of the end of your index finger for the nose.

2. With a sharp knife, carefully cut out the circle.

You will need: *Ball-point pen*
Styrofoam cup
Knife
Yarn
Glue

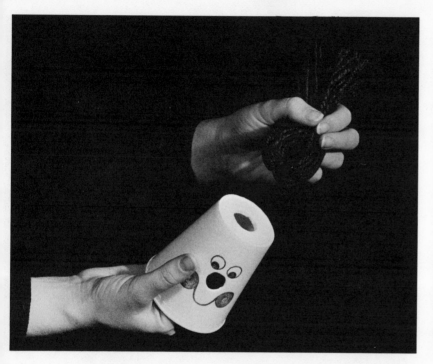

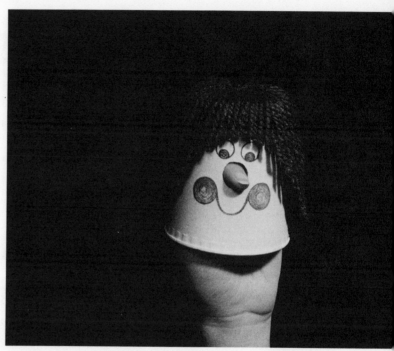

3. Cut a hole in the top of the cup and insert a bundle of tied yarn for the hair.

4. To complete your puppet, glue the hair to the top of the cup and trim it around the face. Insert your hand into the cup so the middle finger becomes a long, moving nose.

31

Box Puppet with Nose-Hole

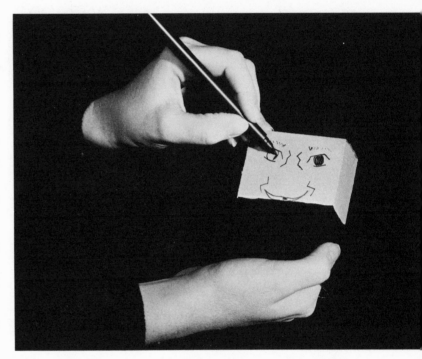

1. Begin by painting a small cereal box any color you choose.

2. Next, with a felt-tip pen, draw on the facial features desired.

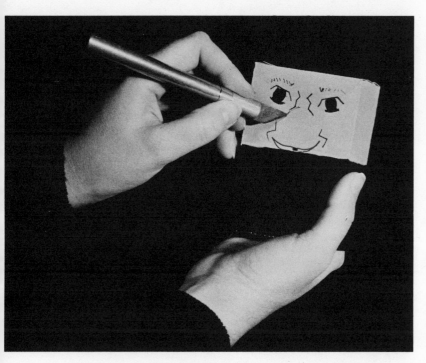

3. Cut a round hole about the size of your index finger for the nose.

4. Add some hair and a hat, both made of construction paper. Hold your puppet so the index finger protrudes through the hole, forming the puppet's nose.

33

Styrofoam Ball Puppet

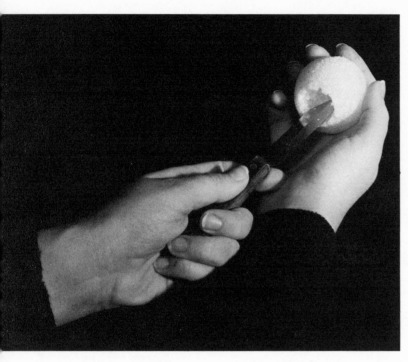

1. In a 2″ styrofoam ball, cut a hole large enough for your index finger.

2. Decorate the ball with plastic eyes; yarn hair; felt mouth, nose, and cheeks; and a hat made of felt and a cotton ball.

You will need: 2″ styrofoam ball   Yarn
Knife   Felt
White glue   Cotton ball
Plastic eyes   Handkerchief

3. Drape a handkerchief over your hand.
Insert your index finger into the head
and your puppet is complete.

Painted Tube Puppet

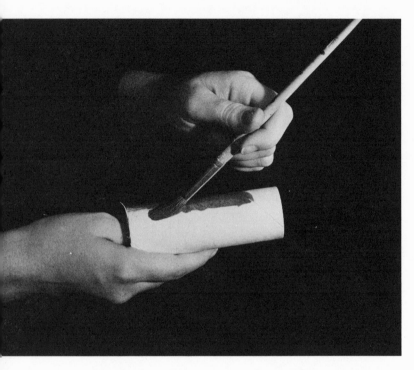

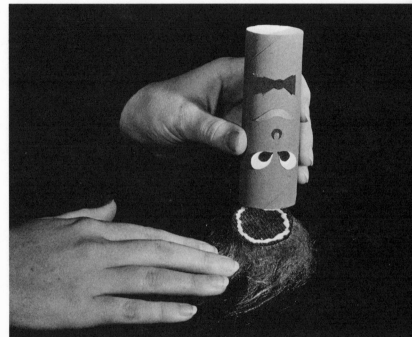

1. Paint a toilet paper tube with tempera paint.

2. Make facial features of construction paper and add them on. Make the hair by cutting a circle of long fake fur and gluing it to the top of the tube.

You will need: Toilet paper tube   Fake fur
                    Tempera paint   White glue
                    Paintbrush   Scissors
                    Construction paper

3. Place your first two fingers inside the
   tube to control the puppet.

Tube Puppet with Holes

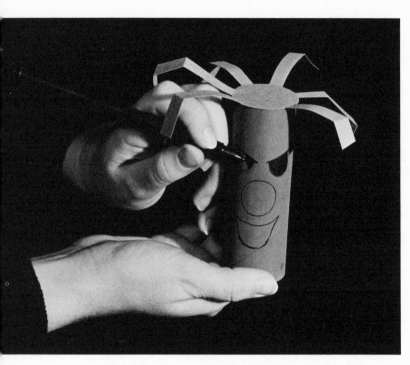

1. Paint and decorate a toilet paper tube to resemble a monster. (We made this monster's hair of construction paper.)

2. With a sharp knife, carefully cut openings for the nose and mouth.

You will need: Toilet paper tube   Felt marker
                       Tempera paint   Construction paper
                       Paintbrush   Knife

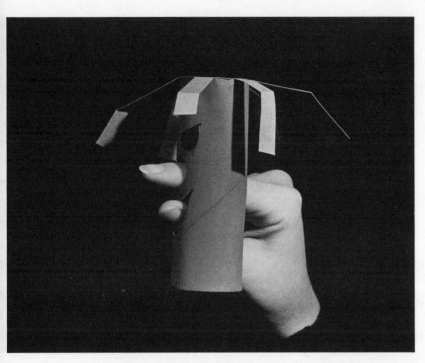

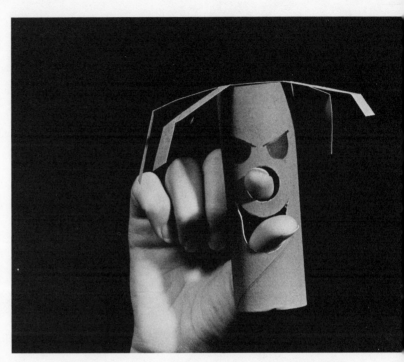

3. Make a slot in the back of the tube. Stick your index finger and thumb through the slots as shown in the photograph above.

4. Your finger becomes the nose and the thumb becomes the tongue to give this puppet a scary appearance.

Tube Dragon

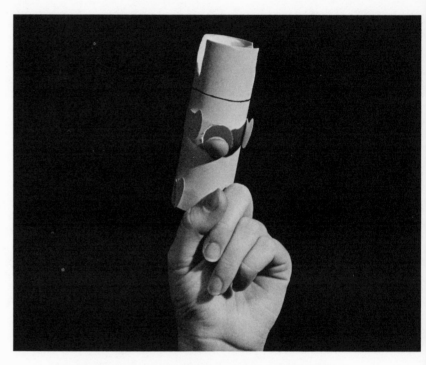

1. Begin by painting a toilet paper tube. Decorate it with felt markers and construction paper. Make the mouth by cutting a notch out of both sides of the tube. Then cut a hole in the underneath side for the index finger.

You will need: Toilet paper tube   Felt markers
                      Tempera paint   Construction paper
                      Paintbrush   Knife

2. Insert your finger, and the puppet is now ready for action.

41

Construction Paper Dancer Puppet

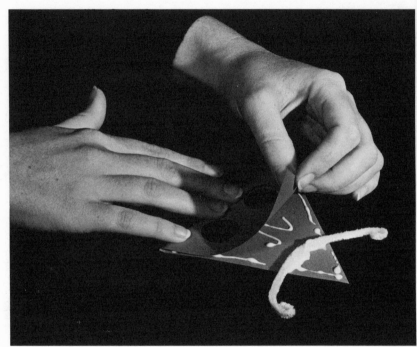

1. First, make tagboard duplicates of patterns 3 and 4. Use tagboard pattern 3 to trace two triangular pieces on construction paper. Cut them out. (This will be the body.)

2. For the arms, place a pipe cleaner between the triangle pieces near the point above the holes. Glue the triangle pieces together.

You will need: Tagboard   Pipe cleaner
Pen   White glue
Construction paper   Felt marker
Scissors

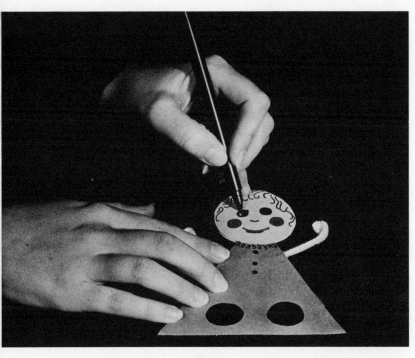

3. Now, use tagboard pattern 4 to trace a circle on construction paper. (This is the head.) Cut out the circle and glue it to the body. Then, using a felt marker, draw a face on it.

4. Complete the puppet by placing your first two fingers through the holes to form the legs.

Felt Dancer Puppet

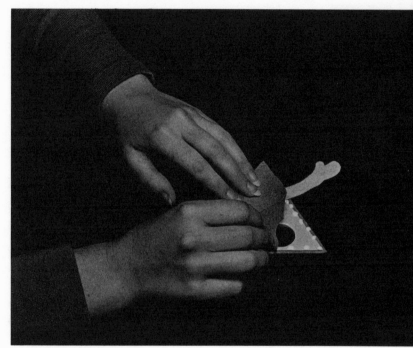

1. Make tagboard duplicates of patterns 3, 4, and 5. Use pattern 3 to trace two triangles with holes on felt and one on posterboard. Next, use pattern 4 to trace two circles on felt and one on posterboard. Make the posterboard pieces approximately ⅛″ smaller than the felt pieces. Cut out all the pieces.

2. Using pattern 5, trace and cut out two pieces of felt for the arms. Place the felt arms on the posterboard triangle and glue on. Now, glue one felt triangle to each side of the posterboard.

You will need: Tagboard   Scissors
Pen   White glue
Felt   Fringe
Posterboard

3. Form the head by gluing one felt circle to each side of the posterboard circle. Glue the head to the body.

4. Complete the puppet by adding fringe for the dress decoration and felt pieces for the hair and facial features.

One-Finger Elephant

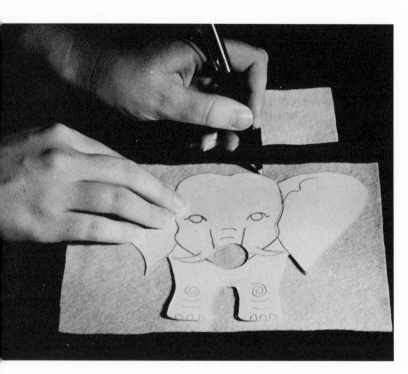

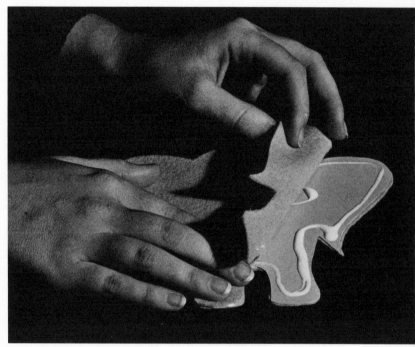

1. Make a tagboard duplicate of pattern 6. Use it to trace two of the pattern outline on felt and one on posterboard. (*Note:* Make the posterboard piece approximately ⅛″ smaller than the felt pieces.) Cut them out.

2. Glue one piece of felt to each side of the posterboard piece. Glue the edges of the felt so the posterboard does not show.

You will need: Tagboard   Scissors
                                    Pen   White glue
                                    Felt   Felt-tip pen
                                    Posterboard   Plastic eyes

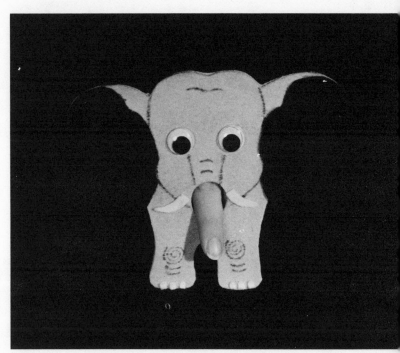

3. Use a felt-tip pen to draw the features. Add large pieces of dark felt to accent the ears. Complete the face with plastic eyes.

4. Stick your index finger through the hole to form the trunk and the elephant is ready to perform.

One-Piece Finger Puppet

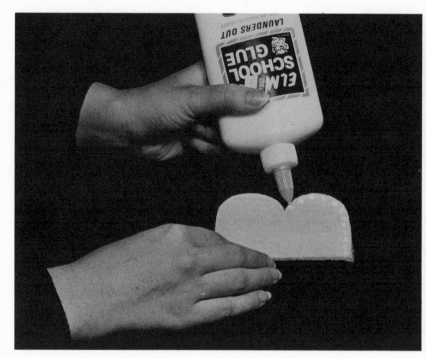

1. Make a tagboard duplicate of pattern 7. Trace the pattern outline onto the reverse side of a piece of fake fur and cut it out.

2. Apply the glue in small dots to one half of the curved edge of the reverse side of the fur. *Do not glue the bottom.*

You will need: *Tagboard*   *Fake fur*
                     Pen   *White glue*
                     Scissors   *Felt*

3. Fold the fur piece over so the fur is on the outside and press the curved edges together.

4. When the glue is dry, add facial features cut from small bits of colored felt.

Cucumber Puppet

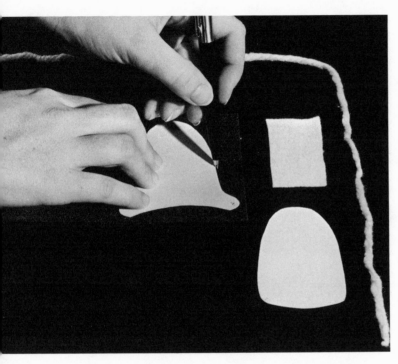

1. Make tagboard patterns from patterns 8 and 9. After tracing the pattern outlines onto pieces of felt, cut them out and glue the pieces together.

2. Using a yarn or rug needle, thread a short length of yarn (approximately 4″) through the top of the head.

You will need: Tagboard   Yarn
                      Pen   Rug or yarn needle
                      Scissors   Felt
                      White glue

3. Cut out several more small strips of yarn (approximately 12) and place them on the head of the puppet. Tie the threaded length of yarn around the smaller strips.

4. Fluff the yarn up for the hair and the puppet is complete.

51

Flat Finger Puppet

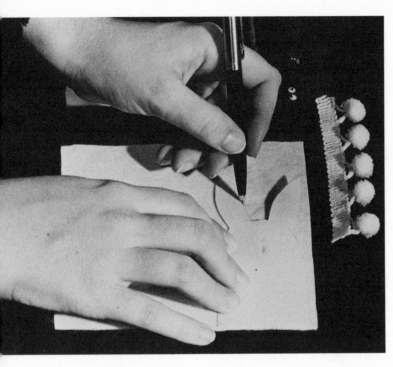

1. Make a tagboard duplicate of pattern 10. Use it to trace two of the pattern outline onto the felt. Cut out the two pieces of felt.

2. Next, apply the glue to the edges of one piece of felt. Use only dots of glue as a solid line will make the material too stiff.

You will need: Tagboard
Pen
Scissors
Felt
White glue

Plastic eyes
Fringe ball
Yarn
Dazzle bead

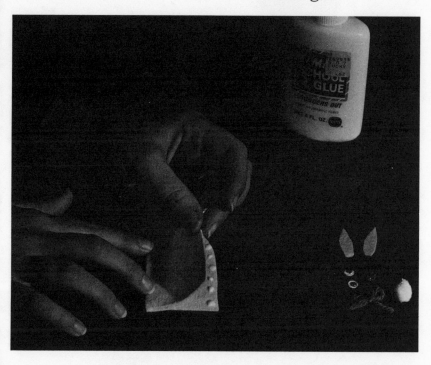

3. Place the felt pieces together and press firmly.

4. Complete the puppet by adding appropriate features: eyes, nose, bow-tie, etc. Also add a fringe ball on back side of puppet for a tail.

Flat Finger Puppet with Separate Head

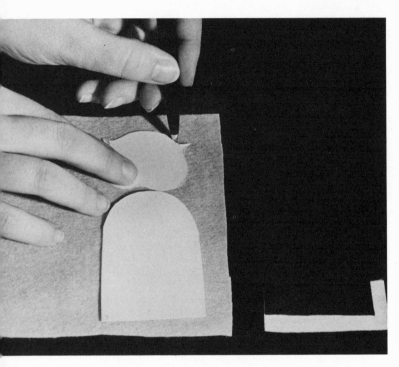

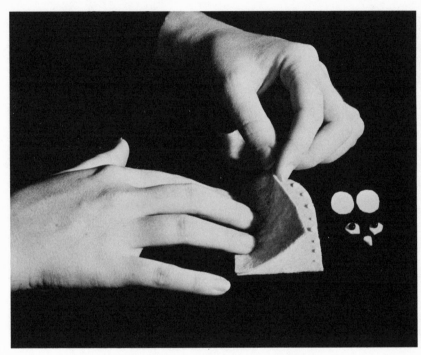

1. Make tagboard duplicates of patterns 11 and 12. Use them to trace the pattern outlines onto the felt. Cut out two pieces of felt in the shape of pattern 11. Cut out one piece of felt in the shape of pattern 12.

2. Glue the long curved edge of the two body pieces together, leaving the bottom edge open.

You will need: Tagboard   Felt
                                   Pen   White glue
                                   Scissors   Dazzle bead

3. Glue the head to the body.

4. Add the appropriate features to complete the puppet. (*Note:* The head of the owl in this photograph uses two different shades of brown felt.)

Variations: By simply changing the design of the head, an almost infinite number of human and animal figures can be created.

55

Stuffed-Head Puppet

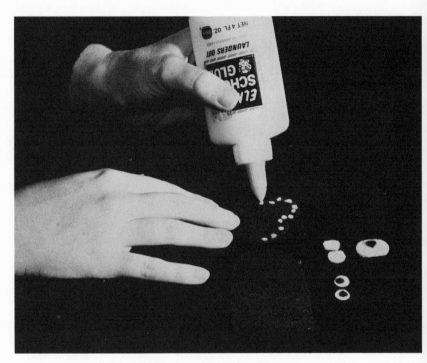

1. Make tagboard duplicates of patterns 11 and 13. Use them to trace the pattern outlines onto the felt. Cut out two pieces of felt for each pattern piece.

2. Glue the head pieces together one half the way around. Use small dots of glue. Let sit until dry, approximately twenty to thirty minutes. Meanwhile, glue the body pieces together, except for the bottom (straight) edge.

You will need: Tagboard
Pen
Scissors
Felt

White glue
Cotton
Plastic eyes

3. After the glue dries, stuff the head with cotton and finish gluing the head together. The head is now ready to be glued to the body.

4. Add the desired facial trimmings to complete the puppet.

Large Body Flat Finger Puppet

1. Make tagboard duplicates of patterns 14, 15, and 16. Use them to trace the pattern outlines onto the felt. Cut out two pieces of each pattern on white felt.

2. Glue the pieces cut from pattern 14 together to form an inner body. Leave a small slit for your finger at the base of the body. Next, place the inner body between the outer body pieces (pattern 15), and glue the edges, except the small slit at the base.

You will need: Tagboard
Pen
Scissors
Felt in white, black,
    and other colors

White glue
Cotton

3. Glue the head pieces (pattern 16) halfway around and let dry. After drying, lightly stuff with cotton. Finish gluing the head pieces together, and attach the head to the body.

4. Make a tagboard duplicate of pattern 17. Use it to cut out a piece of black felt for the snowman's hat. To finish snowman, cut out other appropriate decorations from felt and glue them on.

Finger Puppet with Integral Arms

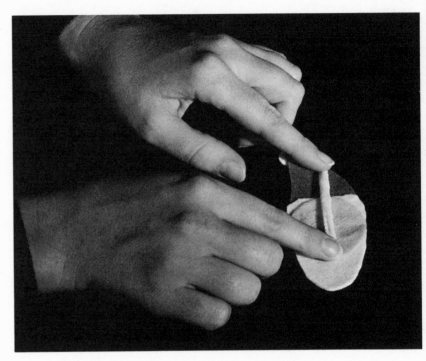

1. Make tagboard duplicates of patterns 18 and 19. Cut out two pieces of felt in the shape of pattern 18. Apply the glue in small dots around the edge of one piece, *except at the bottom,* and glue the pieces together.

2. Using pattern 19, cut out one piece of pink felt for the head. Make the additional features, beard, hair, and cap from appropriate colors of felt (see photograph 4). Glue a pipe cleaner to the back of the felt for stiffness.

You will need: Tagboard White glue
Pen Felt in various colors
Scissors Pipe cleaner

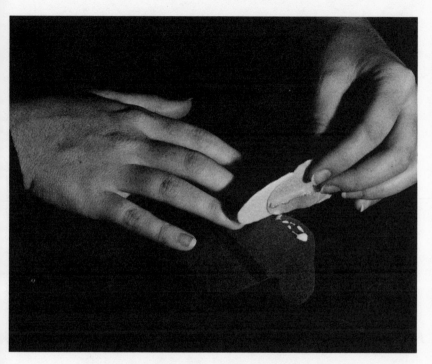

3. Now, glue the head to the body.

4. Insert your finger into the opening in the bottom of the puppet to complete.

Finger Puppet with Separate Arms

1. Make tagboard duplicates of patterns 11, 20 and 21. Cut out four pieces of felt in the shape of pattern 21. Glue the pieces together in sets of two with a piece of pipe cleaner in between for stiffness.

2. Next, cut out two pieces of felt in the shape of pattern 11. Insert the arms between these body pieces. Glue body together along the edges, except at the bottom.

You will need: Tagboard   White glue
                     Pen   Pipe cleaner
                     Scissors   Plastic eyes
                     Felt   Dazzle beads

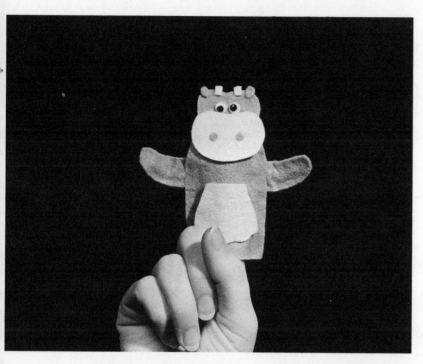

3. For the head, cut out one piece of felt in the shape of pattern 20. Attach the head to the body and add appropriate felt features to complete the puppet.

Side Finger Puppet

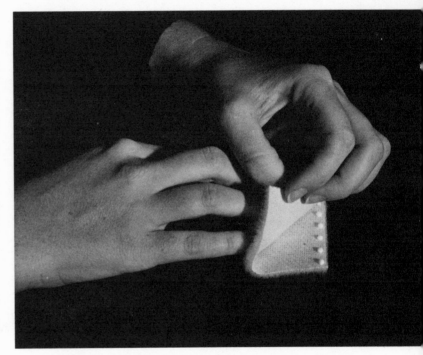

1. Make a tagboard duplicate of pattern 22. Trace the pattern on a piece of fake fur and cut it out.

2. Fold the piece of fur over, furry side out, and glue the sides together using small dots of glue. Leave the end open for your finger.

You will need: Tagboard   Glue
                  Pen   Pink felt
                  Scissors   Fringe ball
                  Fake fur   Dazzle bead

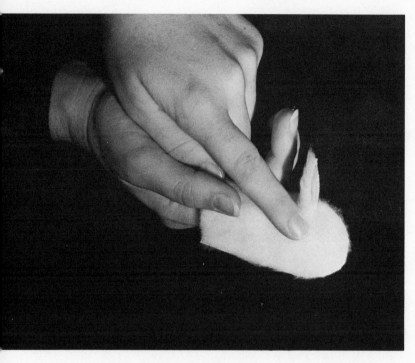

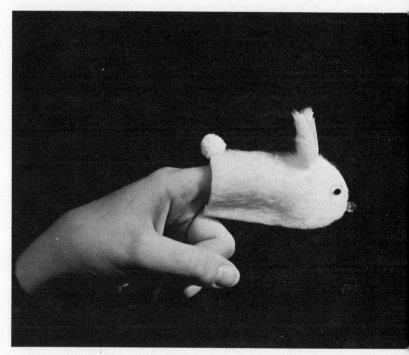

3. Next, cut out two small pieces of fur in the shape of rabbit ears and glue them to the body. Line the ears with pink felt.

4. Add fringe ball for a tail, dazzle bead for a nose, and plastic eyes to complete the puppet.

Cone Puppet

1. Make tagboard duplicates of patterns 23 and 25. Trace one of each pattern outline onto felt and cut out the felt pieces.

2. Shape the large piece (pattern 23) into a cone and glue the edges together.

You will need: *Tagboard*   *Felt*
                  Pen   *White glue*
                  Scissors   *Fringe balls*

3. Glue a fringe ball to the top of the cone to form the lion's head. Attach the piece of felt from pattern 25, which represents the lion's mane.

4. Complete the lion by adding small fringe balls for his paws and pieces of felt for his eyes and nose.

67

Cone Puppet with Stuffed Head

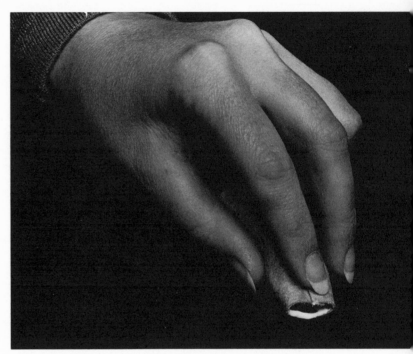

1. Make tagboard duplicates of patterns 23 and 24. Cut out one piece of felt in the shape of pattern 23. Cut out two pieces of felt in the shape of pattern 24.

2. With the large piece of felt (pattern 23), form a cone shape and glue the overlapping edges together. Glue the small end of the cone together also.

You will need: Tagboard   Cotton
                     Pen   Yarn
                     Scissors   Rickrack
                     Felt   Decorative tape
                     White glue

3. Glue the circular pieces (pattern 24) halfway around and let dry. After drying, stuff with cotton and finish gluing together. When dry, glue the head to the small end of the cone.

4. Use felt for the facial features, yarn for the hair, and a strip of decorative tape to adorn the body.

Stuffed Doll Puppet

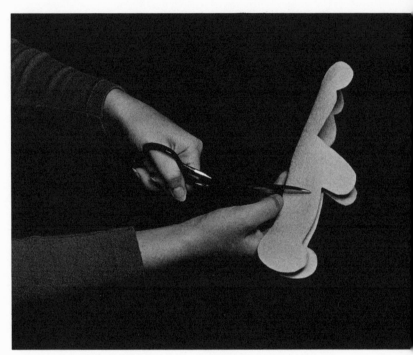

1. Make a tagboard duplicate of pattern 26. Trace two of the pattern outline onto the felt and cut out the pieces.

2. In one of the pieces, cut a straight slit running along the waistline to within ¼″ of each side. Now, glue the two pieces together along the edge, stuffing all of the area above the slit with cotton. Be sure to glue the area immediately above the slit so no cotton can escape.

You will need: Tagboard
Pen
Scissors
Felt
Ruler

White glue
Cotton
Pencil
Plastic eyes

3. Using a pencil, push the cotton down into the puppet's feet.

4. Complete the puppet by adding plastic eyes and facial features of felt. Insert your first and middle fingers into the slit and down the puppet's legs to make it perform.

Hand
Puppets

Thumb and First-Finger Puppet

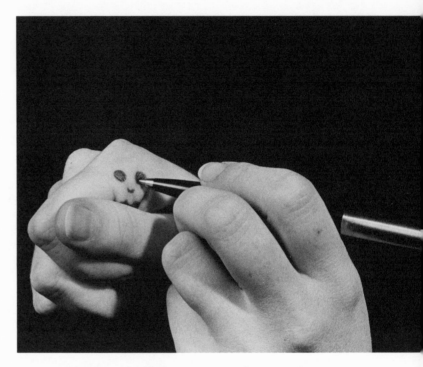

1. Using a ball-point pen, draw a face on your hand similar to the one shown above.

2. Move your thumb up and down to simulate the mouth movement.

Envelope Puppet

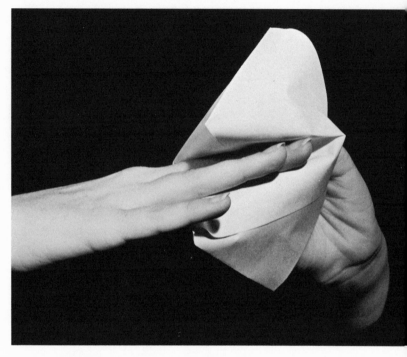

1. Take an envelope, tuck the flap inside, and hold it as shown.

2. With the other hand, press on the bottom crease, causing the two lower corners to meet and form a beak.

You will need: *Envelope*
Felt marker

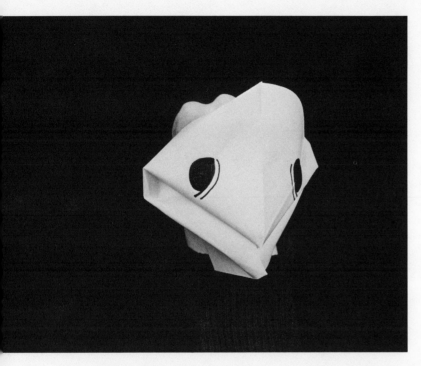

3. With one hand still inside the envelope, use the other hand to draw the eyes. Your puppet is complete.

Shadow Puppet

1. Focus the light from a slide projector on a white wall. Standing a few feet from the wall, arrange your hands to form images on the wall behind you. Experiment with one or both hands to create lifelike shadows. The one shown here is of a bird taking flight.

You will need: *Slide or movie projector*
                                 White wall or screen

Simple Paper Plate Puppet

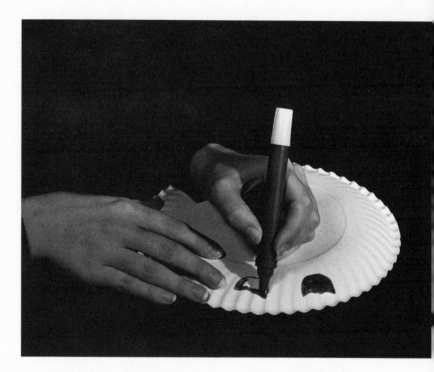

1. With a felt-tip marker, draw two eyes on the back of a paper plate near the rim.

You will need: Paper plate
Felt-tip pen or marker

2. Curve the plate over so the rim forms the mouth. Be careful not to crease the paper plate, as this will cause a loss of springiness and make the puppet difficult to operate.

Elaborate Paper Plate Puppet

1. Cut a paper plate in half.

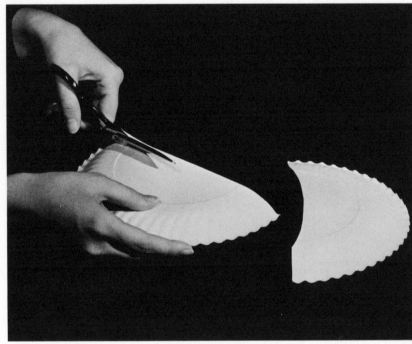

2. Next, cut a curved slice from the straight side of each half.

You will need: *Paper plates*   *White glue*
                        Scissors   *Paintbrush*
                        Tempera paint   *Staples*
                        Felt   *Stapler*
                        Fringe balls

3. Staple the halves to the back side of another paper plate.

4. Cover the two half-plates with paint and decorate the puppet inside and out. Fold the uncut plate in half and slip your hand into the pockets formed by the half-plates. Move your hand up and down to make the puppet talk.

Paper Bag Puppet

1. Paper lunch bags make excellent puppets when the bottom of the bag is folded flat against one side. To operate: Slide your hand to the top of the bag and put your fingers into the fold. The puppet in this photograph is decorated with felt-tip pens.

2. This puppet uses construction paper for its facial features.

You will need: Lunch bags   Cotton
                     Felt-tip pens   Scissors
                     Construction paper   White glue

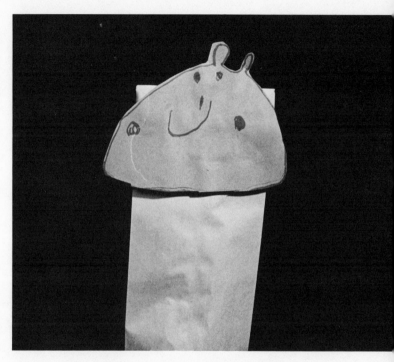

3. The Santa bag puppet is made with large pieces of construction paper for the body, face, and hat. The beard is cotton-covered construction paper.

4. The puppet in this photograph is a bear designed and executed by a four-year-old child.

Creeping Glove Puppet

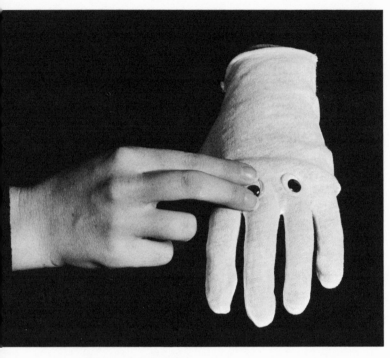

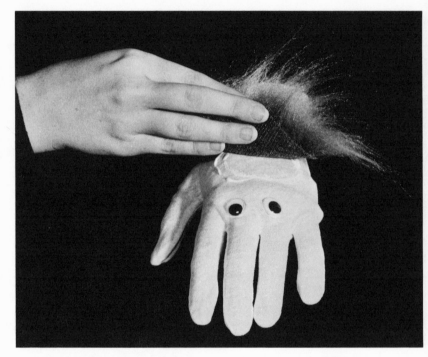

1. Glue two plastic eyes to a white cotton glove just above the middle two fingers.

2. Next, glue a piece of fake fur to the part of the glove covering the back of the hand.

You will need: *White cotton glove*
Plastic eyes
White glue
Fake fur

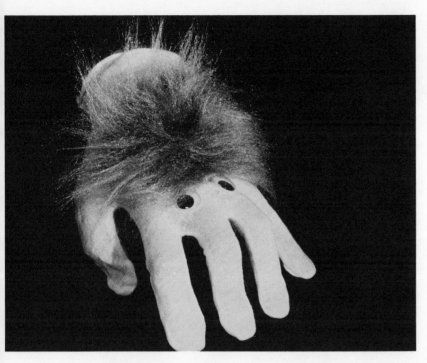

3. Using all five fingers, make this puppet creep across the table.

Crepe Paper Puppet

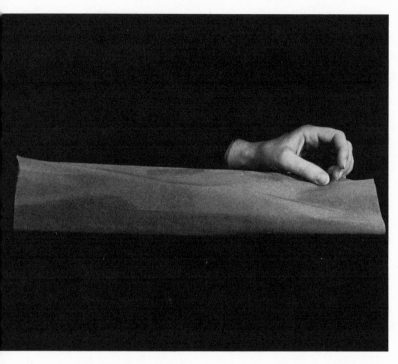

1. Wrap a piece of crepe paper around your arm to form a tube. Tape the overlapping edges together.

2. Fold over ½″ of one end of the crepe paper tube and tape it closed.

You will need: Crepe paper
Construction paper
Scissors
Scotch tape

3. Make a head from a piece of construction paper and attach it to the closed end of the tube.

4. Add other pieces of construction paper to form the puppet's features.

Stuffed Head Paper Bag Puppet

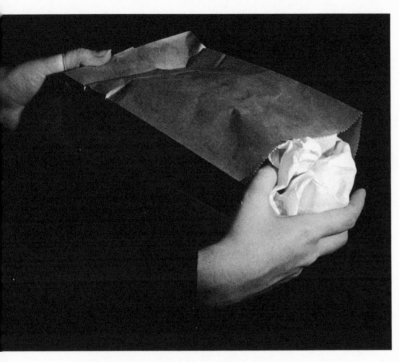

1. Loosely crumple six or seven paper towels and place into an empty paper bag. (An equivalent amount of newspaper may be substituted for the paper towels.)

2. Next, insert an empty toilet tissue tube into the bag. Bunch the bag around the tube and secure it with a rubber band.

You will need: *Paper bag (lunch-bag size)*   *Toilet tissue tube*
     Rubber band
     Paper towels or newspaper   *Felt marker*

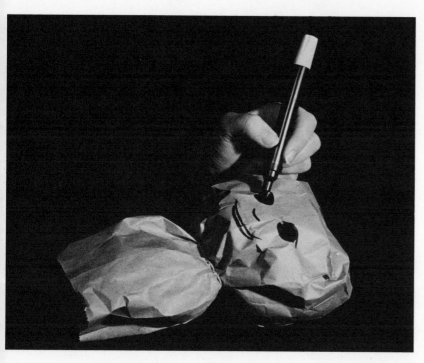

3. With a felt marker, draw on the facial features.

4. Hold the puppet by grasping the toilet tissue tube. Allow the lower portion of the sack to cover your hand.

91

Stuffed Head Paper Bag Puppet with Arms

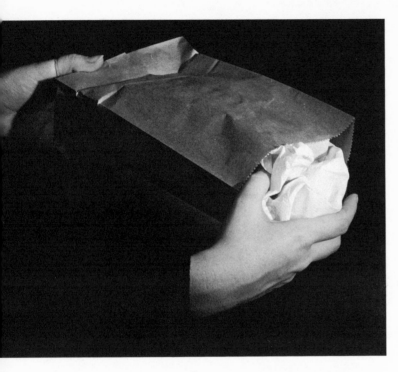 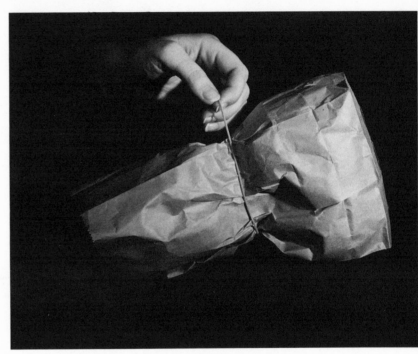

1. Loosely crumple six or seven paper towels and place inside a paper bag.

2. Loop a rubber band around the bag about halfway down. (The bag should fit snugly around your index finger.)

You will need: Paper bag (lunch-bag size)
                       Paper towels or newspaper

Rubber band
Scissors
Felt markers

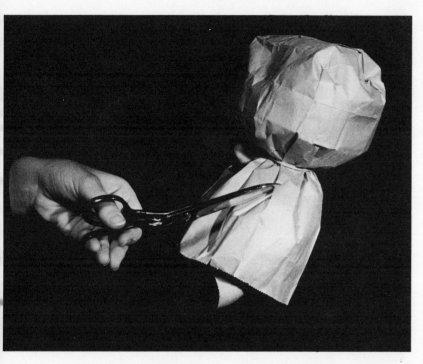

3. Cut a small hole on each side of the sack below the rubber band.

4. Decorate the head with felt markers. Complete the puppet by inserting your index finger into the stuffed portion and allowing your thumb and middle finger to extend through the holes, making arms.

Fruit-Head Hand Puppet

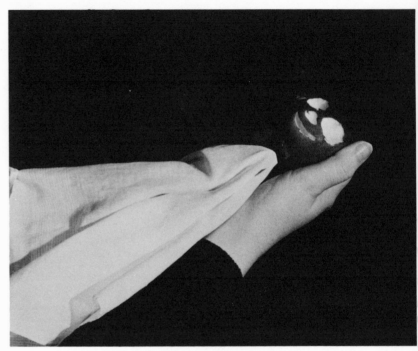

1. With a teaspoon or similar instrument, carve out a face on an apple. (*Note:* A variety of vegetables can be used for the head, e.g.: turnip, potato, zucchini or summer squash, carrot.

2. Next, carve a hole in the bottom of the apple to fit your index finger. Cover your hand with a handkerchief and insert your index finger into the hole.

You will need: Apple
Teaspoon or similar
    instrument
Handkerchief
Rubber band

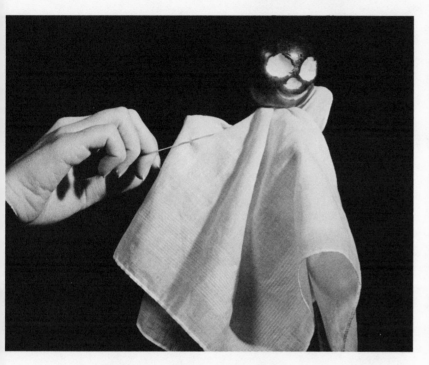

3. With handkerchief still covering your hand, loop a rubber band around your thumb. Pull the rubber band behind your index finger and over your middle finger.

4. To operate your puppet, use the thumb and middle finger as arms.

Traditional Hand Puppet

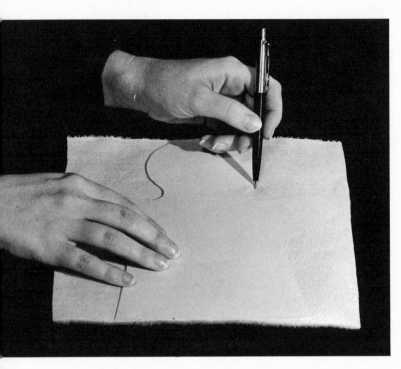

1. Make a tagboard duplicate of pattern 27. Cut out two pieces of fake fur in the shape of the pattern.

2. Place the glue in small dots around the edges of one piece, *except at the bottom*. Place the other piece on top, and press firmly.

You will need: Tagboard   Fake fur
                      Pen or pencil   Glue
                      Scissors   Felt

3. Add felt pieces for the hat, facial fea-
    tures, and body decorations.

Traditional Hand Puppet with Separate Head

1. Make a tagboard duplicate of pattern 28. Cut out two pieces of felt in the shape of the pattern. Glue the two pieces together by putting glue in dots all around the edges, except at the bottom.

2. Make a tagboard duplicate of pattern 29. Cut out two pieces of felt in the shape of pattern 29.

You will need: *Tagboard*   *Felt*
                             Pen   *White glue*
                             Scissors   *Pipe cleaner*

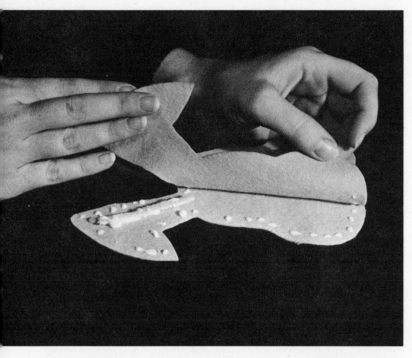

3. Glue the two head pieces together, including pipe cleaner in the ears for added stiffness.

4. Glue the head to the body and add appropriate felt pieces for decoration.

Traditional Hand Puppet with Stuffed Head

1. Make a tagboard duplicate of pattern 28. Cut out two pieces of felt, following the tagboard pattern. Then, glue the two pieces together along the edge, except at the bottom.

2. Make a tagboard duplicate of pattern 30. Cut out two pieces of felt in the shape of pattern 30. Glue the pieces halfway around. Let them sit until dry. Then stuff with cotton and finish gluing together to form the head.

You will need: *Tagboard*   *Felt*
                                   Pen   *White glue*
                                   Scissors   *Cotton*

3. Now, add felt pieces to complete the puppet, which has a realistic three-dimensional effect.

Cereal Box Puppet

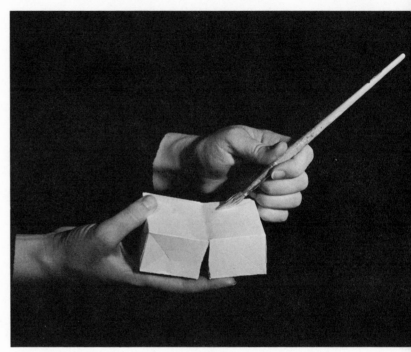

1. Begin by cutting three sides of a small cereal box.

2. Paint the box an appropriate color, using tempera paint.

You will need: Cereal box (variety-
                      pack size)
                      Knife
                      Tempera paint
                      Paintbrush

White glue
Felt
Fringe balls
Plastic eyes
Construction paper

3. After the paint dries, fold the box in half, allowing the ends to form the face. Use felt, fringe balls, plastic eyes, and construction paper to complete the head and facial decorations.

4. Insert your hand into the open side of the box. Move your hand up and down to make the puppet speak.

103

Caterpillar Arm Puppet

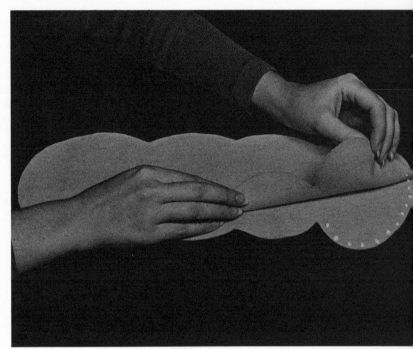

1. Make a tagboard duplicate of pattern 31. Use it to trace the pattern outline onto the felt. Cut out two pieces of felt in the shape of the pattern.

2. Glue these two pieces together along the top and front edge only.

104

You will need: Tagboard   Felt
                      Pen   White glue
                      Scissors   Pipe cleaners

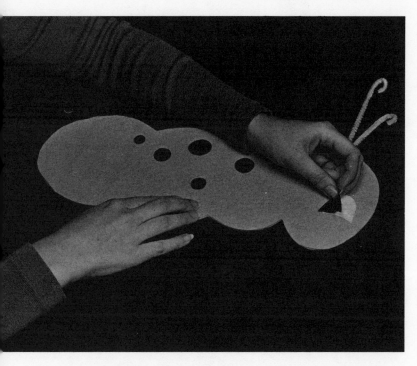

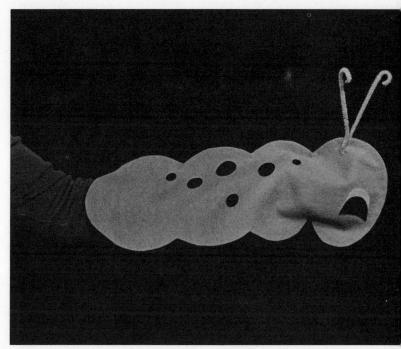

3. Attach pipe cleaners for the feelers and decorate the body with felt spots and eyes.

4. Use this puppet by draping it over your arm with the hand in the caterpillar's head.

Unslit Sock Puppet

1. Glue plastic eyes and felt eyelashes onto an old tube sock near the toe.

2. Next, place your hand and arm inside the tube sock. With your other hand, press between the thumb and hand to help form the mouth.

You will need: Tube sock
White glue
Plastic eyes
Felt

3. The completed puppet should look similar to the one shown here.

Unslit Sock Puppet with Mouth

1. Start with a tube sock. Cut two ovals of felt about twice as long as the sock is wide, and slightly wider than the sock. Cut one posterboard oval slightly smaller than those of the felt. Next, glue the felt ovals together, with the posterboard oval in between to add stiffness.

2. While the glue is still wet, fold the construction to make a mouth. Glue the mouth to the sock, allowing the mouth to overlap the end of the sock by ½″ to ¾″.

108

3. Add eyes and the puppet is ready for use.

Slit Sock Puppet

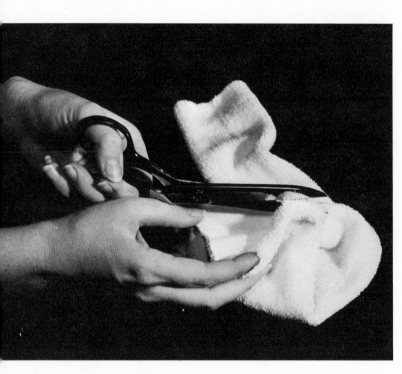 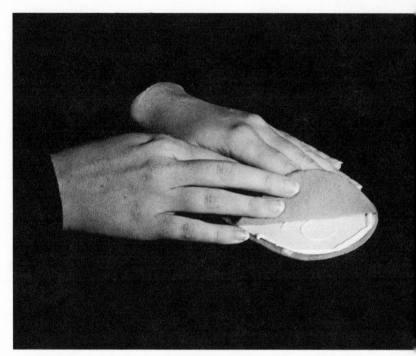

1. Slit the rounded toe of a tube sock from side to side.

2. Next, cut out two ovals of felt about twice as long as the sock is wide, and slightly wider than the sock. Cut out one posterboard oval slightly smaller than the felt ovals. Now, glue the posterboard oval to one of the felt ovals. Place the other felt oval over the posterboard and glue the construction together.

You will need: Tube sock   Posterboard
Scissors   White glue
Felt   Plastic eyes

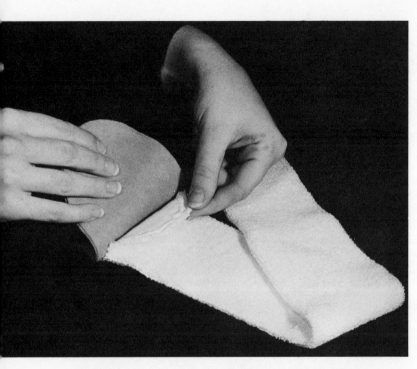

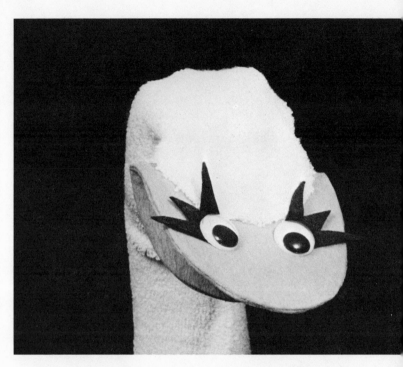

3. While the glue is still wet, fold the construction in half to form a mouth. Place the mouth into the open slit of the sock and glue it to the sock on both sides of the fold. Be careful to apply the glue *only to the very edge of the sock slit.*

4. Add plastic eyes and other desired features to complete the puppet.

Stuffed Sock Puppet

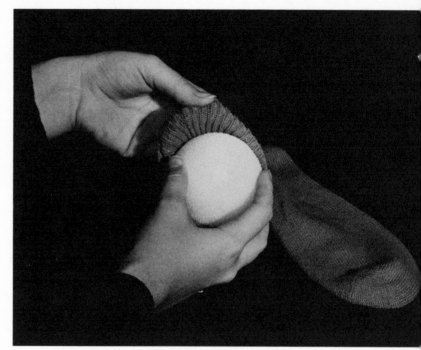

1. With a sharp knife, cut a hole large enough for your index finger in a 3″ styrofoam ball.

2. Insert the styrofoam ball into a sock until it rests in the heel with the hole pointed toward the top of the sock.

You will need: Knife   Felt
                     3″ styrofoam ball   White glue
                     Sock   Fringe ball

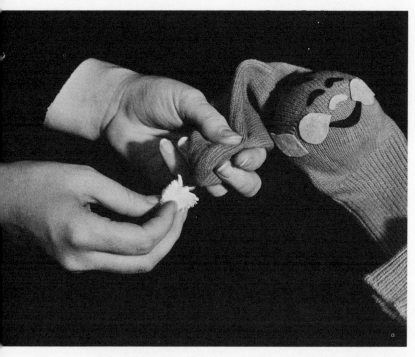

3. Decorate the heel of the sock with felt pieces. Add a fringe ball to the toe of the sock.

4. Flipped jauntily to the side of the face, the toe of the sock becomes an elf's long pointed hat. To manipulate the puppet, place your hand inside the sock with your index finger in the hole.

Silent Puppet

 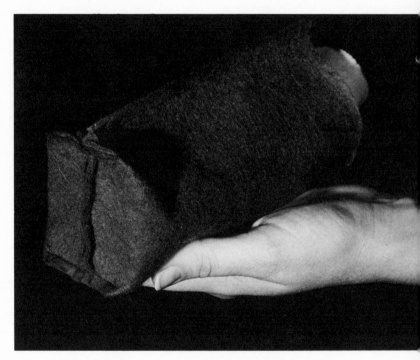

1. Make a tagboard duplicate of pattern 32. Mark pattern letters on your duplicate. Trace the pattern outline onto a piece of felt and cut it out.·

2. Fold the cut-out felt in half lengthwise. First, sew the long edge together from A to B; then sew the short edge from C to D. Refold material so B and C meet, and stitch from E to F. Repeat on other side, matching D to X and stitching from Y to Z. Before turning it right side out, the construction should look like the one shown here.

You will need: Tagboard   Needle
                     Felt   Thread
                     Pen   Steam or dry iron
                     Scissors   Plastic eyes

3. Turn the puppet right side out and fold the top over so it looks like the one shown here. Press the fold in with an iron.

4. Add eyes and your puppet is ready to use. Operate the puppet by sliding your hand to the top of the bag and putting your fingers into the fold.

Can Puppet

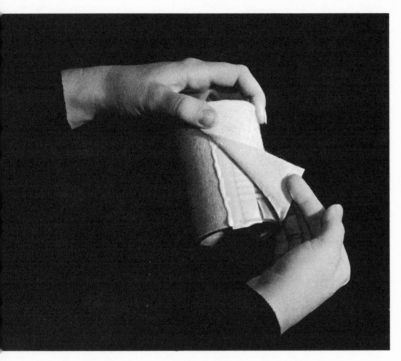 

1. Measure the can you are using. Cut a piece of felt as wide as the can is tall and longer than the can's circumference. Tape one end of the felt to the side of the can. Wrap the felt around and glue it where the pieces overlap.

2. Use a needle and thread to put gathers along the edge of a piece of cloth 8″ by 18″.

You will need:

Can
Felt
Scissors
White glue

Cloth 8″ x 18″
Needle and thread
Yarn
Rickrack

3. Wrap the gathered edge of the cloth around the can and glue it in place. Also glue the cloth together all along the edge where it meets.

4. Glue yarn hair to the top of the can and felt features to the face. Complete the puppet by tying a piece of rickrack around the dress. (*Note:* This puppet may also be made using a toilet paper tube instead of a can.)

Slipper Puppet

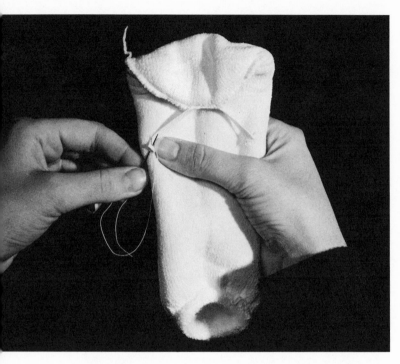

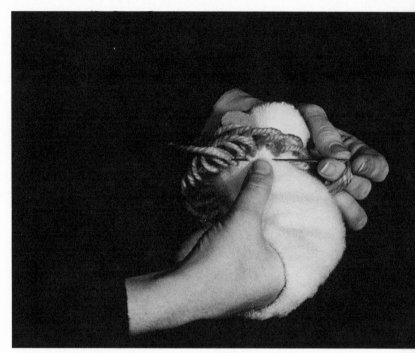

1. Begin with a soft cloth slipper turned wrong side out. With a needle and thread, attach a short length of elastic to the toe and to each side, as shown here. Turn the slipper right side out. The elastic should pull the cloth in to form a mouth.

2. Make a lion's mane by threading loops of yarn through the slipper all around the toe. (Also see photograph of completed puppet in step 3.)

You will need: Soft cloth slipper
Needle and thread
Elastic
Yarn

Felt
Plastic eyes
Scissors
White glue

3. Use pieces of felt for the features and add plastic eyes to complete the puppet.

About the Patterns

In the following pages you will find patterns you will need for making some of the puppets in this book. We have used one side of the page only for printing the patterns so you can cut them out if you wish. We suggest that you make tagboard duplicates of the patterns so that they will last through repeated use. If you cut the patterns from this book, you may either trace the outlines onto the tagboard and cut them out, or glue the patterns onto the tagboard and cut around them. If you wish to leave the patterns in the book, use tracing paper to copy the outlines; then proceed as above.

Remember, you can create your own pattern variations and make tagboard duplicates for them also.

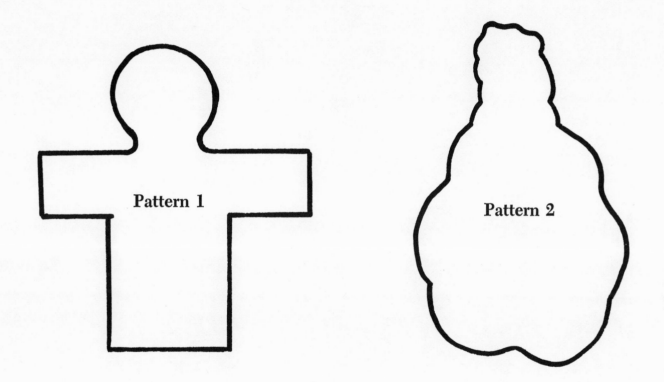

Pattern 1

Pattern 2

121

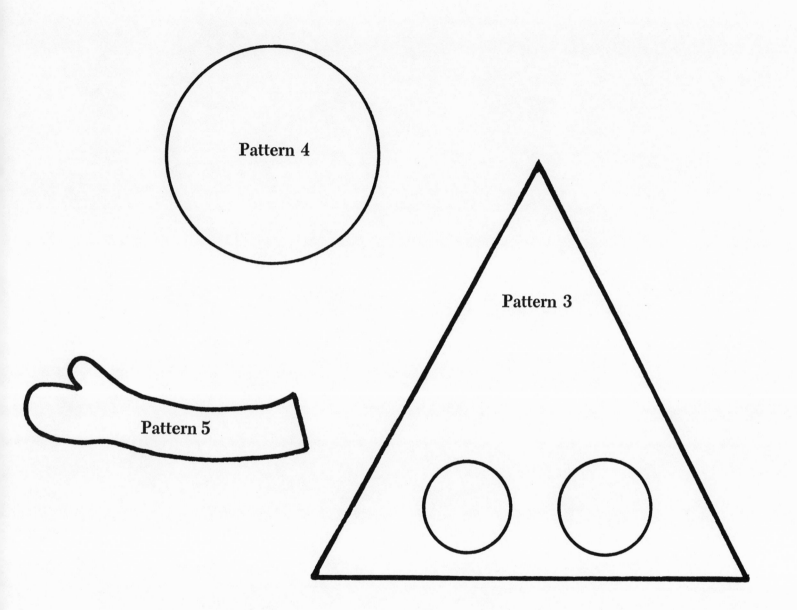

Pattern 4

Pattern 5

Pattern 3

123

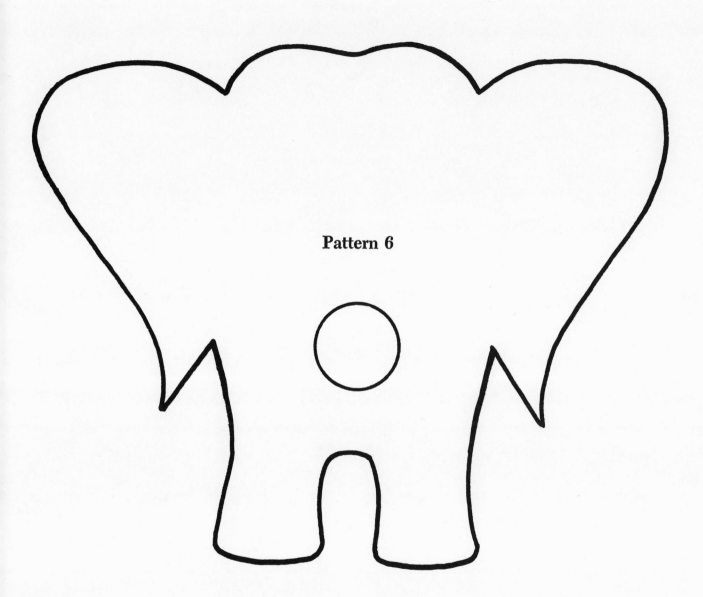

Pattern 6

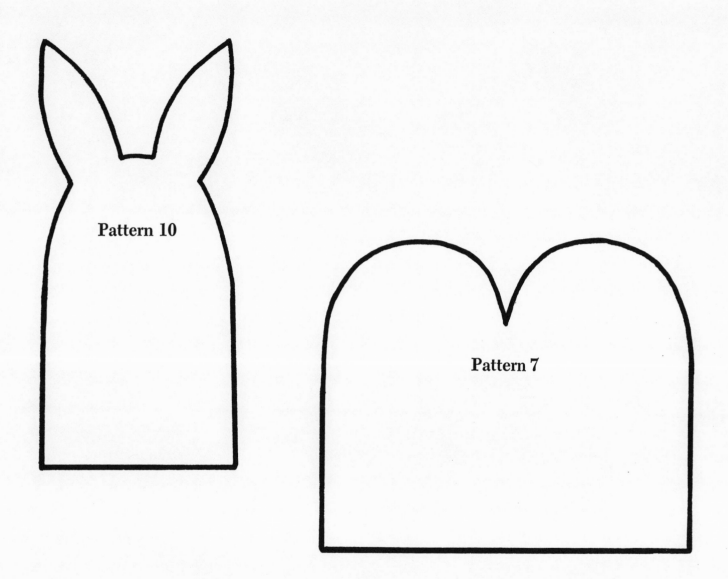

Pattern 10

Pattern 7

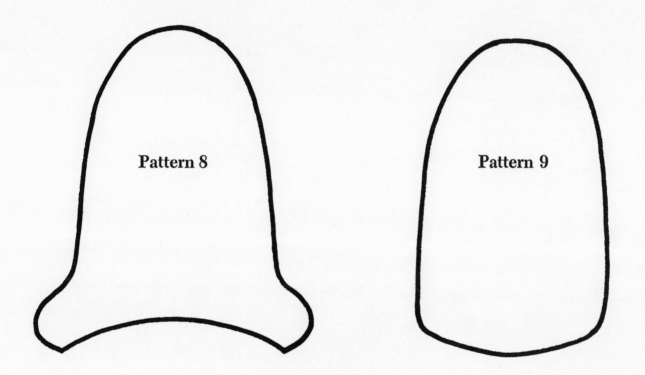

Pattern 8

Pattern 9

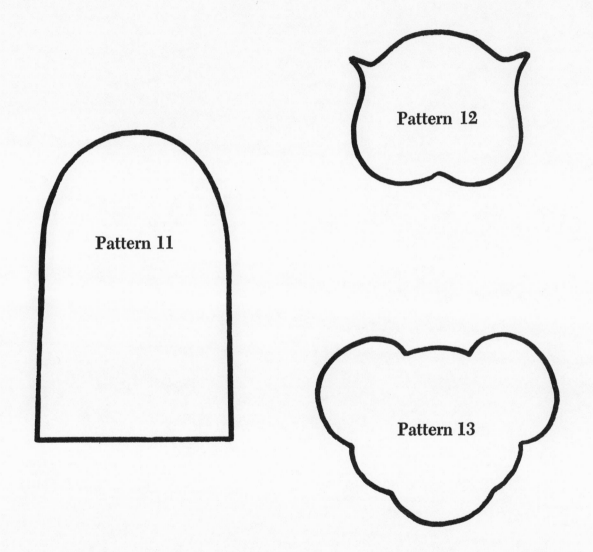

Pattern 11

Pattern 12

Pattern 13

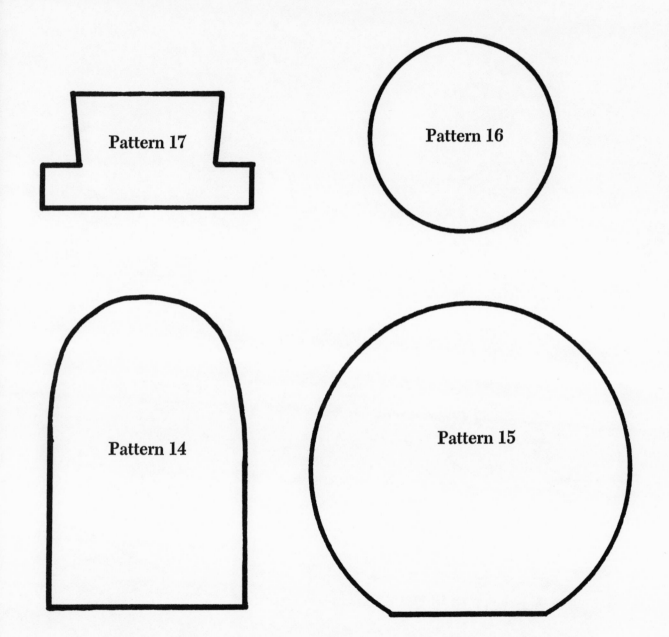

Pattern 17

Pattern 16

Pattern 14

Pattern 15

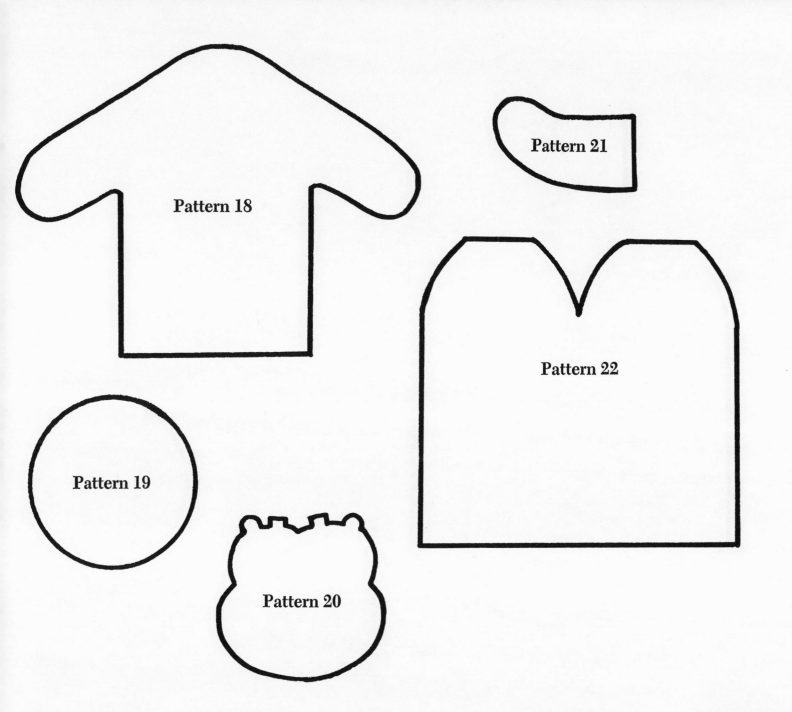

Pattern 18

Pattern 21

Pattern 22

Pattern 19

Pattern 20

135

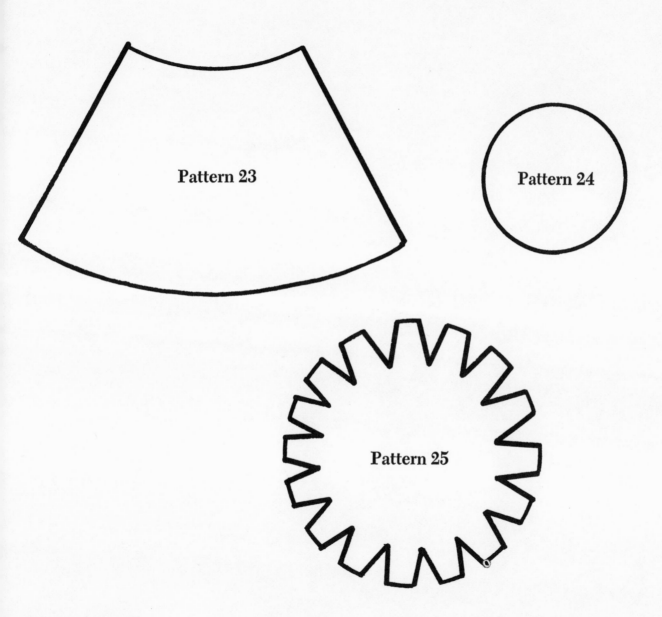

Pattern 23

Pattern 24

Pattern 25

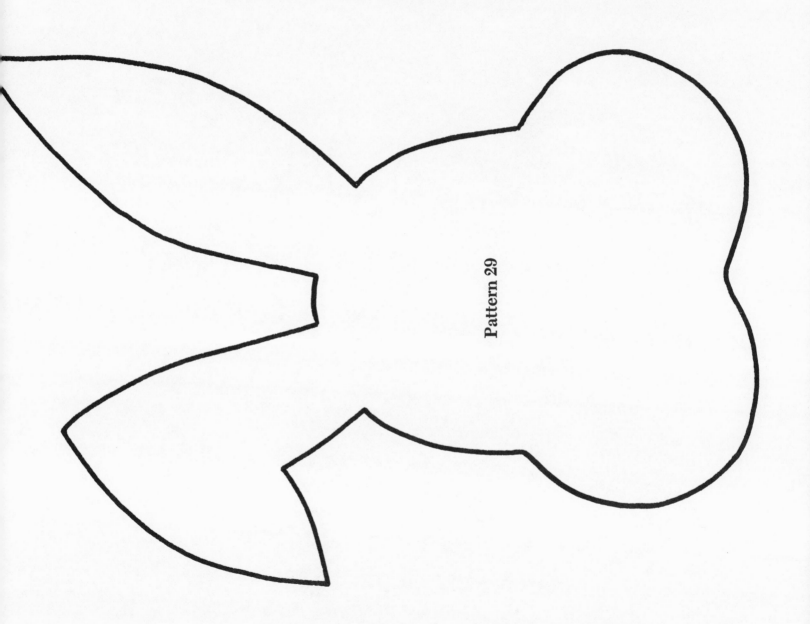

Pattern 29

139

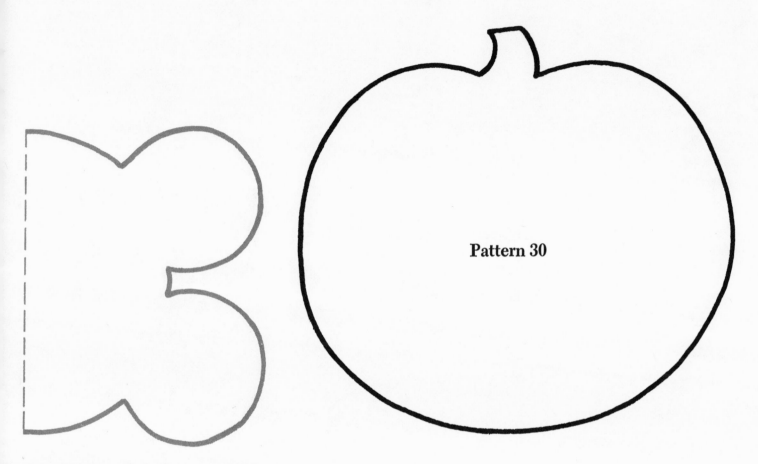

Pattern 30

IMPORTANT: Do not cut into this part of the page. Part of Pattern 26 is printed on the reverse side, as shown by the grey outline.

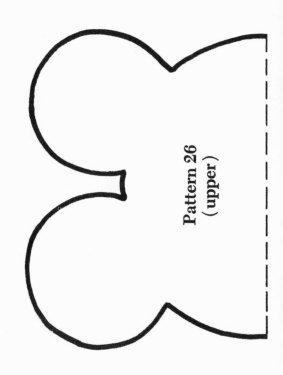

Pattern 26
(upper)

This pattern is too large to fit on one page. Cut out the two sections and tape them together at the dotted line. Your completed pattern should look like this small outline.

142

Pattern 26
(lower)

143

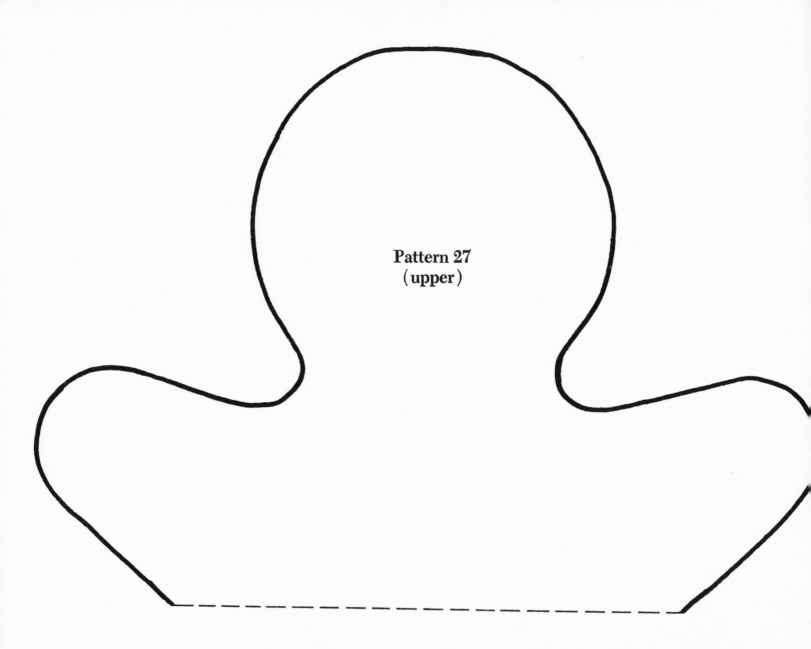

Pattern 27
(upper)

146

This pattern is too large to fit on one page. Cut out the two sections and tape them together at the dotted line. Your completed pattern should look like this small outline.

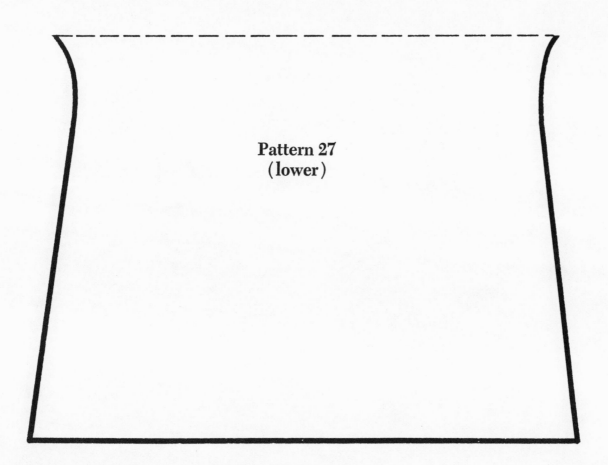

**Pattern 27
(lower)**

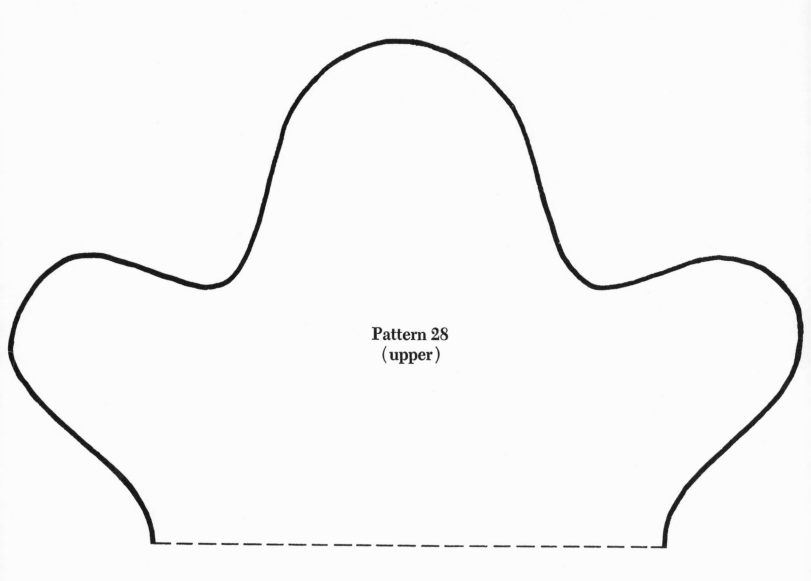

Pattern 28
(upper)

150

This pattern is too large to fit on one page. Cut out the two sections and tape them together at the dotted line. Your completed pattern should look like this small outline.

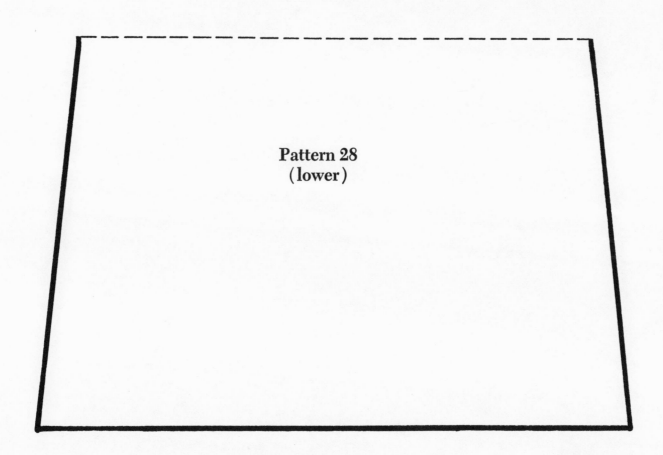

Pattern 28
(lower)

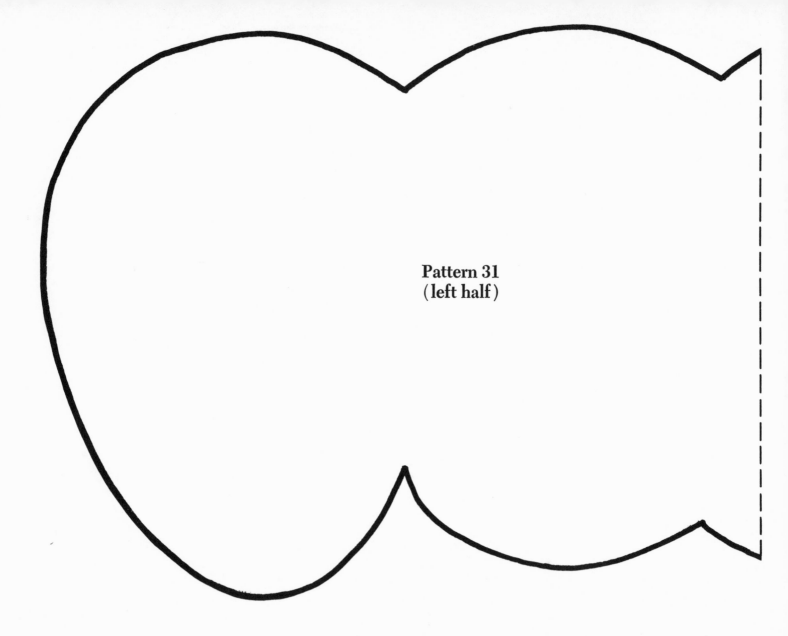

Pattern 31
(left half)

This pattern is too large to fit on one page. Cut out the two sections and tape them together at the dotted line. Your completed pattern should look like this small outline.

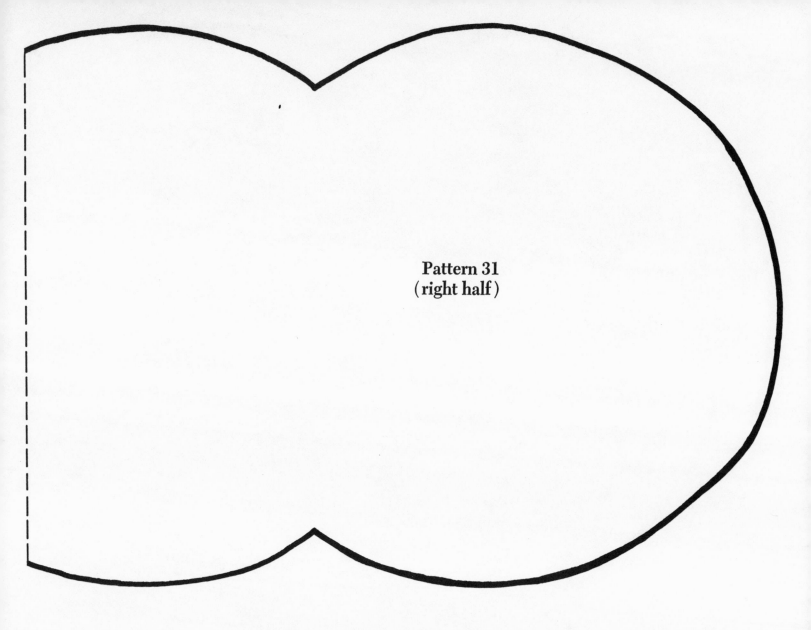

Pattern 31
(right half)

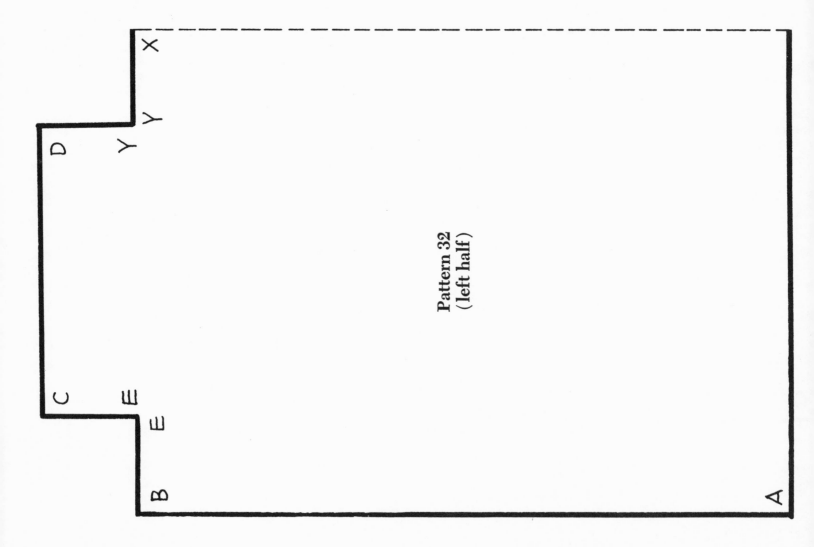

Pattern 32
(left half)

158

This pattern is too large to fit on one page. Cut out the two sections and tape them together at the dotted line. Your completed pattern should look like this small outline.

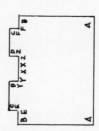

Pattern 32
(right half)